My BIG BOOK of Bible Stories

VOLUME FOUR

In him was life, and that life was the light of men.
John 1:4 NIV

© 2011 by Phil A. Smouse
ISBN 9781729219270

Oh, not again. Just what we need—
a thousand porky piglets freed!
A mile-long sausage-link stampede,
hog-wild and crazy guaranteed!

He must be here. He's back in town.
Yes, every time He comes around
this town just seems to come undone.
Just LOOK—here comes another one!

OH, NOT AGAIN!

That man was *lame!* How strange. How odd.
He's walking—leaping—praising God!
And over THERE! Oh, fear! Oh, dread!
Last week that guy right there was *dead!*

How can this BE? I have to see
this man from up in Galilee!
What's that? You want to see Him, too?
Okay. Let's go. I'll follow *you!*

Who am I? What do I do?
I'm Nicodemus. Who are you?
What's THAT? That's my phylactery.
You see, I am a *Pharisee.*

A Phari-WHO? A Pharisee!
And who, pray tell, or what is he?
Well, if you listen carefully,
I'm sure that soon, you'll start to see.

It started quite some time ago,
and I was there, so I should know!
I saw it all. The shame—*disgrace*—
at Matthew, the tax-collector's, place. . .

That place? Oh dear! The scent. The smell!
And, *oh my word*—the clientele!
I've never seen a meaner bunch
all gathered up for Sunday brunch.

The house was packed with thugs and brutes
and folks with bad and ill-reputes.
Hoodlums! Gangsters! Outlaws! Cads!
Villains, rogues, and crooks—*EEEGADS!*

And there among the bums and brutes,
the rascals, thugs, and big-galoots,
sat *JESUS!* Eating—laughing—talking!
Loving! Teaching! Shameful! SHOCKING!

Dirty hands and dirty feet.
Dirty things to drink and eat!
Dirty hearts and dirty heads—
He didn't mind. He *loved* instead!

Now as you know, or may have guessed,
that left my heart a bit distressed.

And so, that night, without a peep,
once everyone had gone to sleep,
I slipped out on my hands and knees
and tip-toed through the tulip trees—

beneath the stars, there by the sea,
I met the man from Galilee!

I looked at Him. He looked at me.
His eyes were meek and *wild* and free.
It seemed to me like He could see
right through the hardest Pharisee!

He reached deep down inside my heart
and gently filled up every part.
I didn't know quite what to say,
but oh, it came out anyway.

"Jesus, please—before you go,
there's one small thing I have to know.

It's clear that you've been sent by God,
for *who* could doubt, the way You've awed,
amazed, astonished, and impressed us—
honored, cherished, loved, and blessed us!

Changed the water into wine—
healed the sick time after time—
raised men up from in the grave. . .
But, what must I DO to be saved?"

"Oh, *THAT'S* easy," Jesus said.
No need to kneel or bow your head.
For God to live inside, My friend,"
He said, *"You must be born again!"*

BORN again! BORN AGAIN?
How can a man be BORN again?
That will not work. That does not wash.
Not here, or in Oshkosh, b'gosh!

How can a man so big and smelly
get back in his mommy's belly?
Should I, could I, if I would?
I WOULD NOT, even if I could!

I would not sleep inside a crib,
or eat my breakfast with a bib,
or dribble oatmeal down my chin.
NO! I CAN NOT be born AGAIN!

Wear a pair of baby-booties?
Dress in lace and tootie-fruities?

Take my bath inside the sink,
all shriveled, wrinkled-up, and pink,
while everyone begins to shout,
'Let's go and get our cameras out!'

OH NO, I WON'T!
NOT ME. NO WAY—

No matter what You do or say!

I will not wear a big, fat Huggie,
ride inside a baby buggy,
rub-a dub or splish and splash,
then get a case of diaper-rash!

I can not do the thing you say.
The thing you say *is not okay!*
Not here. Not there. Not now. Not then.
No, I CAN NOT be BORN AGAIN!"

"Oh, Nicodemus," Jesus said,
"I don't mean born *like that* again.
Your outsides are just fine, My friend.
Your HEART—*that* must be born again.

For God so loved this world that He
gave up His only Son—*that's Me!*
and all who trust Me deep inside
will LIVE and never, ever die!"

"I AM the Way. The Truth. The Life.
The First. The Last. Yes, Jesus Christ.

Behold, I stand—I stand and knock,
and wait for you to come unlock
the door that leads into your heart—
the door that's keeping us apart.

Please let me give MY life to you.
Oh, that is what I long to do!"

So do I did. Well, wouldn't you?
Of course you would! You'd do it, too!
You'd let Him in right on the spot.
You'd say, "Okay! Of course! Why not!"

My soul was clean. My sins were crushed!
My stone-cold heart was corn-meal-mushed.
I once was blind, but now I see—
For Jesus lives *inside of me!*

THE PARABLE OF THE VINEYARD WORKERS

Matthew 20: 1-16

"The first shall be last and the last shall be first!"

So, you think that the words must have gotten reversed?
Well, I'll tell you a secret: that's what I thought, too!
Oh, but not anymore—and soon *neither will YOU!*

A man had a vineyard. An honest, fair man.
And this honest, fair man really needed a hand. . .

"I'll give you all one whole denarius each,
if you're willing to work," he besought and beseeched,
"in my fields for the day, where you'll trudge and you'll traipse
back and forth, up and down, as you harvest my grapes."

Now, *one whole denarius,* that was some loot,
just for trudging and traipsing, and picking up fruit.
"We've all hit the jackpot!" the workers yahoodled.
"To pass up THIS deal would be out-of-your noodled!"

So work they all did. Yes, they picked and they plucked.
They scooted and scampered and toted and trucked.
They gave thanks to the Lord for their awesome good-lucks,
for quite soon they'd be making the big, mega-bucks.

They worked very hard. Yes, they gave it their best.
They all huffed and they puffed without taking a rest.
But they couldn't keep up, so right back into town
went that honest, fair man to see who could be found
that would rather be working than standing around.

He went back there at nine, noon, and three on the dot.
Yes, he went back FOUR times—to the very same spot.
And every last time he'd just give the same speech:
"One whole, bright, shiny denarius each!"
and they'd run for his field just like kids at the beach.

Oh, and wouldn't you know, they got all the work done.
Yes the plucked every grape out there under the sun.
And that honest, fair man was as pleased as could be.
They had done what they said, and now, yes—*so would he!*

"What a beautiful, wonderful sight," thought the man.
"Every ONE worked *so hard*—now I think that we can
call it quits for the day, and with that I will say,
'It was fun. Thanks a ton. Come and pick up your pay.'"

"Call up the paymaster. Give them their dough.
Tell them all *thank you*, and then they can go.
Line them all up so the last ones are first,
and give them their one-tiny, bright-shiny, mine-finally
pure-silver coin so they're all reimbursed."

Now, one whole denarius, that was some loot,
just for trudging and traipsing and picking up fruit.
But the men who were hired way back at the first
were beginning to think that THEIR deal was *the worst!*

"Now listen here mister, we started at *dawn!*
You're paying these *new guys* the same? Oh, come on!
"We've been robbed!" they all shouted. "We huffed and we puffed,
and now what do we get? We get *not-near enoughed!*

Well, that honest, fair man knew those men were upset.
But he gave every man what he said they would get.
So he opened his heart. He had something to say.
And the thing that *he said* really blew them away!

"I gave EACH OF YOU what I said you would get,
and *I know you worked hard,* but don't ever forget—
I NEVER said those who worked *more* were the best.
I give all men the same. No one more—no one LESS."

"God's love can't be earned. If it could, we would boast.
He loves all men the same. He loves no man the most!"

You can bop till you drop. That's okay, but it's true:
It will never depend upon how much you do.
When you come unto Him, *He will come unto you. . .*

That's a pretty good deal, I would say. Wouldn't you?

"I HAVE A STRANGE TALE.

I have a strange tale I've been meaning to tell,
about a young fellow I know fairly well.
And so, if you've got a spare minute or two,
I'd be ever so happy to tell it to YOU!

How strange could it be? Oh, come on—you know ME.
It's as strange as a tale could impossibly be!

"Hey Pop," I exploded, "wake up and get dressed.
I've got a few things to get off of my chest!"

"I've had ALL I can stand. I can't stand any more!
This place is the pits. It's a snooze. It's a bore.
I'm a-gettin' on out while the gettin' is good,
and I'm not looking back 'til I reach Hollywood!

And oh yes, by the way— if you'd do me ONE favor,
it really *would* be a tremendous time-saver—
all that money you said that I'd get you-know-when,
well I want it RIGHT NOW! So go get it, amen?"

Well, to my great surprise, he forked over the loot.
And he did it without a bark, peep, or hoot.
So I packed up my bags and I ran for the hills.
I ran for the fun and the sun and the thrills!

I did my own thing. Man, I had it my way.
It was wall-to-wall, non-stop, just-do-it. Hooray!
It was wild. It was great. It was way-cool, far-out. . .

Right on up to the point where the money ran out!

Well, I got pretty hungry. I needed some food.
So I got me a job with a farmer-type dude,
who said, "I've got the thing for you here, Mr. Big—
you'll be feeding this awful green stuff to my pig."

"To your PIG?" I inquired. "That's why you were hired!
So do it right now," he up-heaved, *"or you're fired!"*
So, what's the big deal? Just go give him some chow?
Well that's easy for YOU to say, isn't it now!

This pig was no teeny, pink, pork-and-bean weenie.
THIS pig was a curly-tailed, wild-eyed *meanie*—
a big, bad, Tasmanian, pot-bellied sow—
a thousand-pound, honey-glazed ham-hock, and how!

So feed him I did—every night and each day.
I'd ker-plop that green glop and he'd chomp it away—
and I knew if I didn't eat something real soon,
I'd be in there MYSELF with a fork and a spoon.

My stomach was empty. My clothes were a mess.
"Oh, why did I do what I did?" I confessed.
I'm sure that my Father won't take me back now.
I *just* can't see why. No, I just can't see how!

I don't want my room or my robes or my rings.
No, I can't ask for ANY of those kinds of things.
I'M NO LONGER WORTHY OF BEING HIS SON!
Oh, why did I do it? Oh, why did I run!?

I'll ask for a job—just a job—nothing more.
I'll clean out the stable. I'll polish the floor.
I'll take out the trash— yes, I'll even do that.
I'll live out in back, on the porch, with the cat!

That ought to do it. Yes, that's what I'll say.
Then maybe he'll think about letting me stay.

So I packed up my bags and I ran from the hills.
But the thing I saw *next* really gave me the chills!

And the thing that I saw was that FATHER of mine. . .
He was waiting right there for me, all of the time!

"MY SON HAS COME HOME!" There were *tears* in his eyes!
Well, I have to admit, that was quite a surprise.

"Kill our best calf! Make a feast fit for kings!
Go and get my best robe—my best shoes—my best ring!
Everyone! Quickly! Come gather around!
Oh, my son who was lost, my dear SON, *he is found!"*

Well, I learned something then on that day, in that place.
Yes, I learned of my Father's great love and His grace.

And I learned that it's not what you do or you've done,
but I learned that it's *Jesus*—God's only Son—
who's the one and the ONLY one-way to be free. . .

He will take YOU back, too.
Go on—*ask Him!* You'll see!

write to Phil A. Smouse

Once upon a time, Phil A. Smouse wanted to be a scientist.

But scientists don't get wonderful letters and pictures from friends like you. So Phil decided to draw and color instead! He and his wife live in Lancaster Pennsylvania. They have two children they love with all their heart.

Phil loves to tell kids like you all about Jesus. He would love to hear from you today! So get out your markers and crayons and send a letter or a picture to:

phil@philsmouse.com

Or visit his website at http://www.philsmouse.com/

Made in the USA
Monee, IL
11 February 2020